W9-BSU-045

Contents

The Southwest

Native peoples have lived in the Southwest region of North America for thousands of years. This region includes the present-day American states of Arizona, New Mexico, southern Utah, and southern Colorado. It is sometimes called the **Four Corners** because the borders of all four states meet at one point. This region, shown on the map below, includes canyons, mountains, valleys, forests, deserts, **mesas**, and **plateaus**. Its climate can be extremely hot or cold, and the only steady water sources are rivers, such as the Colorado River, the Gila River, and the Rio Grande. The Native peoples thrived despite the area's **arid**, or dry, climate and extreme temperatures because they had a deep understanding of the land and how it could provide for them.

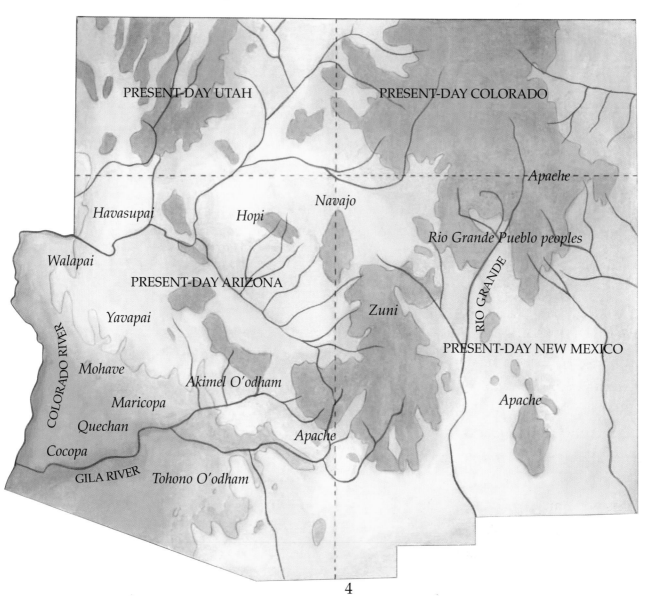

PRESENT-DAY UTAH

PRESENT-DAY COLORADO

Apache

Navajo

Havasupai

Hopi

Rio Grande Pueblo peoples

Walapai

PRESENT-DAY ARIZONA

RIO GRANDE

Yavapai

Zuni

COLORADO RIVER

PRESENT-DAY NEW MEXICO

Mohave

Akimel O'odham

Maricopa

Apache

Quechan

Cocopa

Apache

GILA RIVER *Tohono O'odham*

NATIONS
OF THE
SOUTHWEST

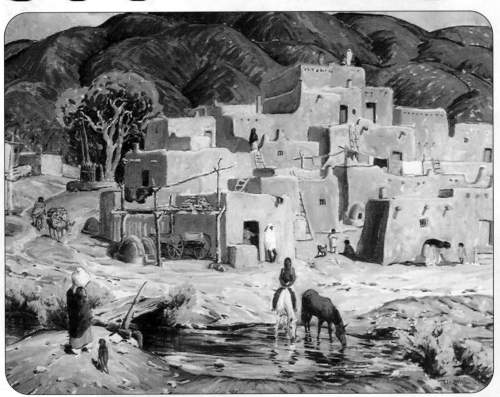

Amanda Bishop & Bobbie Kalman

 Crabtree Publishing Company

www.crabtreebooks.com

NATIONS OF THE SOUTHWEST

Created by Bobbie Kalman

Dedicated by Barbara Bedell—to Bailey, may her love of books grow with her

Editor-in-Chief
Bobbie Kalman

Writing team
Amanda Bishop
Bobbie Kalman

Editorial director
Niki Walker

Editors
Kathryn Smithyman
Rebecca Sjonger

Research
Rebecca Sjonger

Art director
Robert MacGregor

Design
Margaret Amy Salter

Production coordinator
Heather Fitzpatrick

Photo research
Laura Hysert
Jaimie Nathan

Print coordinator
Katherine Berti

Consultants
John D. Gates, J.D. Lecturer, University of New Mexico Native American Studies Department. Enrolled member of the Cheyenne River Sioux Tribe, Eagle Butte, SD.
Rebecca S. Hernandez, Ph.D., Director of Curatorial Affairs, Indian Pueblo Cultural Center, Albuquerque, New Mexico

Photographs and reproductions
© American Museum of Natural History Library: page 11
Circa:Art/Getty Images: pages 1, 12, 13 (top), 26
Courtesy of the Eiteljorg Museum of American Indians and Western Art: *Going to the Waterhole*, Walter Ufer (image trimmed), 5; *Moving Day*, Oscar E. Berninghaus (image trimmed), 8; *The Corn Picker*, Walter Ufer, photo courtesy of Robert Wallace (image trimmed), 9 (top); *Deer Hunter's Camp*, Bert Geer Phillips (image trimmed), 9 (bottom); *Baking Bread*, Victor Higgins (image trimmed), 10
The Greenwich Workshop, Inc. Shelton, CT: © Howard Terpning: *Chased by the Devil* (detail), front cover; *Scouts' Report* (detail), 27; © Tom Lovell: *Pony Tracks and Empty Saddles* (detail), 25; *Coronado's Expedition* (detail), 28
Sherry Harrington: page 31
Nativestock.com: page 30
Alfredo Rodriguez: *Navajo Family*, 22; *Weaving Lesson*, 23; *Shearing Time*, 29
Smithsonian American Art Museum, Washington, DC / Art Resource, NY: pages 13 (bottom), 16, 17
Stark Museum of Art, Orange, Texas: Ernest Martin Hennings, *Returning from the Canyon*, back cover; John Mix Stanley, *The Hieroglyphic Rock of the Gila*, 7 (bottom)
© SuperStock: page 6; © David David Gallery/SuperStock: pages 14-15
© Thomas A. Wiewandt: page 19
All other images by Digital Stock and Corbis Images

Illustrations
Barbara Bedell: pages 18 (top), 20, 21 (bottom), 24 (bottom)
Katherine Berti: page 4
Margaret Amy Salter: border, back cover (hide skin), pages 9, 11 (bottom), 16, 18 (bottom left), 21 (top), 24 (top)
Bonna Rouse: background (pages 1, 14, 15, 17, 18, 24), pages 11 (top), 18 (bottom right)

Crabtree Publishing Company

www.crabtreebooks.com   1-800-387-7650
Copyright © **2003 CRABTREE PUBLISHING COMPANY**.

Printed in the U.S.A./012014/SN20131105

Library of Congress Cataloging-in-Publication Data
Bishop, Amanda.
  Nations of the Southwest / Amanda Bishop & Bobbie Kalman.
    p. cm. -- (The Native nations of North America series)
Includes index.
This book introduces children to the many Native nations of the Southwest region of North America as they lived prior to European contact.
  ISBN 0-7787-0374-6 (RLB) -- ISBN 0-7787-0466-1 (pbk)
  1. Indians of North America--Southwest, New--Juvenile literature. [1. Indians of North America--Southwest, New.]
I. Kalman, Bobbie. Title. III. Series.
  E78.S7B58 2003
  979.2'5901--dc21
                                                    2003001790
                                                          LC

Published in Canada
Crabtree Publishing
616 Welland Ave.
St. Catharines, Ontario
L2M 5V6

Published in the United States
Crabtree Publishing
PMB 59051
350 Fifth Avenue, 59th Floor
New York, New York 10118

Published in the United Kingdom
Crabtree Publishing
Maritime House
Basin Road North, Hove
BN41 1WR

Published in Australia
Crabtree Publishing
3 Charles Street
Coburg North
VIC, 3058

Nations of the Southwest

The Southwest was home to some of the very first people in North America, who are described on pages 6-7. Around the year 1300, their **descendants** began to separate into smaller groups and spread throughout the region. The groups became what are now known as the **nations** of the Southwest. The people of these nations developed cultures that distinguished the nations from one another. They had different languages, homes, customs, traditions, and spiritual beliefs. Each nation also had its own territory, as shown on page 4. This book describes the nations as they lived just before the first Spanish explorers arrived in the early 1500s. Many descendants of these nations continue to live in the region, carrying on their traditions, customs, and languages.

Ancient cultures

The first people in the Southwest were **hunter-gatherers**. They did not live in one place but, instead, followed herds of the animals that they hunted. They also gathered wild plants for food. Eventually, they began growing plants—especially **maize**, or corn—for food. These crops provided a steady supply of food, so people no longer needed to travel in search of plants and animals. The people soon built permanent villages and grew maize, beans, and squash on the land around their homes. During the time they were hunter-gatherers, they came into contact with one another often, but once the groups settled in villages, they no longer met one another on their travels. Over time, each group developed a unique culture and lifestyle, including its own language, crafts, and spiritual beliefs. The largest of these groups were the Anasazi, the Mogollon, and the Hohokam. Some **archaeologists**, or scientists who study ancient peoples, have also identified smaller groups, including the Sinagua, Salado, Patayan, Mimbres, and Casas Grandes, who lived around the same time.

The Anasazi

The people known as the Anasazi thrived for more than a thousand years, until about 1300. At first, the Anasazi lived in **pithouses**, which were dwellings dug into the ground and covered with mats. Around the year 700, these people began to construct buildings above the ground for storage. Soon, they built multilevel, apartment-style buildings with hundreds of rooms to house all the people of a village. These dwellings, such as the one shown opposite, were the first **pueblos**.

The Mogollon

The Mogollon lived for a thousand years along the border of present-day Arizona and New Mexico, until about 1300. They lived in villages of pithouses built close together, which made it easier to defend themselves against enemies. Being skilled farmers, these people raised maize, beans, squash, cotton, and tobacco. They also hunted animals with bows and arrows. The Mogollon were expert basket makers, potters, and weavers.

The Hohokam

The Hohokam people thrived for more than one thousand years, until about 1500. Their name means "vanished ones" in the language of their descendants, the Akimel O'odham. These people lived in villages made up of as many as 100 pithouses. Like the Mogollon people, they raised maize, beans, squash, cotton, and tobacco, and made baskets, pottery, and cloth. They also painted pictures on stone, called **acid etchings**.

Ancient pueblos were often built against rock faces or on cliffs, where they were shaded from the sun and easy to defend against enemies.

*Ancient **petroglyphs**, or etchings on stone, made by people long ago can still be seen today.*

Different lifestyles

The nations of the Southwest had different lifestyles, depending on where they lived. Those who lived near rivers had a steady source of water and were **sedentary** farmers. They lived in permanent villages, farmed near their homes, and made only short trips to gather wild plants or hunt animals. People who lived in areas that had little rainfall and were far from rivers often faced desert-like conditions.

Without a reliable source of water, these people could not raise crops. They were **nomadic**, or traveled constantly within their territories in search of animals to hunt and wild foods to gather. **Seminomadic** nations lived in areas that received rain for a short time each year. They farmed during this time and spent the rest of the year traveling throughout their territories to hunt and gather.

The Southwest nations lived in different landscapes and climates, but each group grew to understand how the land around them could provide everything they needed. People used natural materials such as stones, clay, bones, animal skins, and plant fibers to make shelters, tools, weapons, utensils, and clothing.

Farming

Farmers in the Southwest grew three food crops: beans, squash, and maize. Some also raised tobacco, cotton, melons, and sunflowers. Farmers knew the land well—especially where to find water. Those who lived near rivers sometimes used **irrigation**, or a system of trenches, to direct river water to their fields. **Flood farmers** relied on heavy rains to water flat fields or planted crops near rivers that overflowed their banks each year.

Some Native peoples gave an ear of corn to each newborn baby for good luck.

Hunting

Native people knew where to find animals that would provide meat and other important materials such as bones, hides, and furs. They hunted a variety of animals, including elk, deer, antelope, rabbits, wolves, pumas, coyotes, snakes, lizards, squirrels, wild pigs, and **bison**, or buffalo. Before and after a hunt, Native people always gave thanks to the animals for sacrificing their lives to feed the hunters and their families.

Gathering

People also knew where to find certain plants and how to use them for food or medicine. Groups of gatherers journeyed to find and collect the plants they needed. Cactuses, agaves, yuccas, piñon trees, and juniper trees provided fruits and seeds, and trees such as mesquite, pine, fir, desert willow, and cottonwood provided important materials such as fibers and wood. People crushed seeds such as sunflower seeds to make oil.

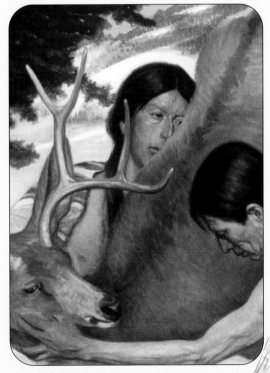

Hunters often used bows and arrows to take down large game such as this deer. When hunting smaller game such as rabbits, hunters used wooden clubs.

Homes in the Southwest

Many types of dwellings were built in the Southwest. People lived in homes that suited their lifestyles. Some homes, such as pueblos, were permanent. Others, such as **wickiups**, were easy to pack up and move from place to place.

Pueblos

The Pueblo peoples were named for the dwellings in which they lived. Their sprawling pueblos sometimes housed whole villages. In fact, the word "pueblo" comes from the Spanish word for "village." Pueblos were built with stones or bricks made of **adobe**— a mixture of clay, straw, and water. People shaped the mixture into bricks and dried them over a fire or in the hot sun. They also used adobe to **plaster**, or cover over, the brick walls of the pueblos. The adobe plaster helped hold the bricks together and gave the walls a smooth finish. Pueblos were sturdy structures that lasted for years.

Shade on the river

Many nations constructed open shelters called **ramadas**. A ramada had a flat roof made of wooden poles woven together with plant fibers. The roof was held up by four wooden posts. Some nations lived in ramadas year-round. Others used them only in the summer months and moved into low, earth-covered dwellings when the weather turned cold. These dwellings were made of pole frames covered with brush and then plastered with mud. A bark mat covered the low doorway to hold in heat.

Hogans

Hogans were dwellings made with wooden poles, bark, and earth. The earliest hogans, such as the one shown right, had cone-shaped frames made of wooden poles. The frames were covered with mud or bark. People added animal hides or blankets to the walls when the weather turned cold.

Later hogans had wooden frames with six or eight sides, domed roofs, and mud walls. The doors always faced east. Many families had hogans in more than one area and moved from one hogan to the next as the seasons changed and animal herds moved.

wickiup

Grass homes

Brush, grasses, and poles were used to make many kinds of dwellings, including wickiups. Wickiups were temporary dwellings that were often used by nomadic peoples and people on hunting-and-gathering trips. These dome-shaped homes had frames of wooden poles that were covered with brush or reed mats. Animal hides were sometimes laid over the coverings to keep the inside of the wickiups warm and dry. The small doors faced east.

Pueblo peoples of the Rio Grande

Many Pueblo peoples lived in villages along the Rio Grande and its **tributaries**. Each village had its own name, such as Taos, Jemez, or Zia. Although the people of the Rio Grande pueblos spoke different languages, they had similar lifestyles. They sometimes hunted, fished, and gathered wild plant foods, but they grew most of their food by farming on rich river banks.

At first, they relied on the river to flood and water their crops, but in later years, the people began directing river water to their farms using irrigation. The Rio Grande's steady supply of water provided good farming through all the seasons, so these peoples were able to live in their homes year-round.

These women of the Taos pueblo are making a short trip to collect water.

Craft making

All Pueblo peoples were well known for their skills of making baskets and pottery. They wove baskets from grass, leaves, roots, and bark and used dyed fibers to make patterns. They also made jars, bowls, and jugs from clay. They often painted their pottery with natural **pigments**, or plant and mineral dyes.

(right) Traders from many nations came to the pueblos to find beautiful goods such as pottery.

Moccasins *were soft, durable shoes stitched from animal hides. People decorated them with beautiful patterns. This man at the Taos pueblo is making moccasins in a variety of styles.*

The Zuni

Another Pueblo group, the Zuni nation, lived in pueblos on the plateaus and mesas west of the Rio Grande. They call themselves the Ashiwi, which means "the flesh." Their villages were usually made up of more than one pueblo. Some village members did not even live in the pueblos but in smaller structures nearby.

Like other Pueblo peoples, the Zuni constructed their pueblos and other buildings around a central **plaza**, or open square. The plaza was an important part of village life. It was used to hold ceremonies, games, and other public events.

This Zuni pueblo had ball courts, where exciting games were held.

A way of life

The Zuni were flood farmers, but they added meat, fruits, and vegetables to their diets by hunting animals and gathering wild plants. Zuni hunters left their villages to catch small animals such as rabbits and badgers. They traveled alone or in small groups, often camping for a few days until they finished a hunt. On rare occasions, groups of Zuni hunters journeyed to hunt bison, shown right, on the **Great Plains**, a vast prairie land to their north.

The Hopi

Members of the Hopi nation lived in pueblos located farther west than those of the Zuni. Their name came from the Hopi word "hopituh," which means "peaceful ones." Like the Zuni, the Hopi were farmers who hunted and gathered to add to their diets. They farmed around their villages on land called the Tutsqua. It was **ancestral homeland**, or land on which their ancestors had lived.

Each family had its own plot of land in the Tutsqua. There was no steady source of water, however, so people depended on rain and flash floods to water crops. The Hopi, along with the other Pueblo peoples, relied most on maize. Maize had long, hardy roots and blue, white, red, and yellow kernels. Corn was so important that it was part of many Hopi religious ceremonies.

This Hopi family uses mules to carry a harvest from the field to their village.

In a pueblo

Like most pueblos, Hopi homes were giant buildings with up to five levels. Each level was slightly smaller than the one below it.

People entered a pueblo by climbing a ladder up to the roof of the first level, as shown above. The upper levels of the dwelling were also connected by ladders.

Farmers of the Gila River

In the villages of the Akimel O'odham and Tohono O'odham, large dwellings were made of willow frames covered with brush and mud.

Carving a history
The Tohono O'odham recorded their history on **calendar sticks**.

Calendar sticks were carved with notches and symbols. These markings represented important events such as battles, ceremonies, and natural disasters.

Two related nations, the Akimel O'odham and Tohono O'odham (formerly known as the Pima and Papago), lived in what is now southern Arizona. They inhabited the territory of their ancestors, the Hohokam. Both groups farmed, although they farmed in different ways. The Akimel O'odham lived along the Gila River and used irrigation, whereas the Tohono O'odham lived deeper in the desert and depended on rain and floods to water their crops. As a result, the Akimel O'odham were also known as "river people," and the Tohono O'odham were known as "desert people."

Village life

Unlike the Akimel O'odham, who lived year-round in one village, the Tohono O'odham had different homes at different times of the year. In summer, they lived on the flat lands where they farmed. After the crops were harvested and the flood waters were gone, the people moved to villages near mountain springs. They kept two sets of everyday items they needed—one at each camp—so they did not have to carry many belongings with them when they moved. When food was especially scarce, many of the Tohono O'odham went to live and work with the Akimel O'odham.

Saguaro fruit

The Akimel O'odham and Tohono O'odham had many uses for the fruit of the giant saguaro cactus. They ate it fresh, dried it for storage, ground it into powder to flavor beverages, made it into jam, and boiled it into syrup to make ceremonial wine. People harvested the fruit using long wooden poles. The traditional harvest of this fruit continues today, as shown above.

Colorado River farmers

The Quechan (Yuma), Mohave (Mojave), Cocopa, and Maricopa nations spoke languages belonging to the Yuman **language family**. They were the largest nations along the Colorado and Gila Rivers. The Mohave and Quechans were aggressive to smaller nations such as the Halchidhoma, Kohuana, Kaveltcadom (Kavelchadom), and Halyikwamai. These groups were eventually taken in by the Maricopa for protection. In time, the smaller nations became part of the Maricopa nation.

The Colorado River farmers raised their crops during the summer, when the rivers flooded their fields of maize, beans, squash, and sunflowers. People grew more food than they needed and stored the extra to use in winter. Some nations lived in permanent villages. Others were seminomadic. They lived in temporary camps of ramadas or earth lodges and moved as seasons changed.

The Quechan beadwork necklace shown above was highly valued and was often used for trade.

When harvests were poor, many nations hunted and gathered wild foods. The Mohave were one of the few Southwest nations that fished to supplement their diets. They were skilled fishers who caught fish with nets and baskets—and even by hand! Most often, the fish was cooked in a stew made with cornmeal. Mohave men used rafts and poles to travel to fishing spots along the Colorado River.

Northern hunter-gatherers

Other Yuman-speaking nations, including the Havasupai, Yavapai, and Walapai (Hualapai), lived in the deserts and on the plateaus of northern Arizona. These nations were not as large as others in the Southwest, but they had big territories. They sometimes farmed, but all three groups were mainly seminomadic hunter-gatherers. The land in their territories was very dry, so they moved with the seasons to find water, plants, and animals to hunt.

Havasupai

The Havasupai, or "people of the blue-green water," lived in what is now called Cataract Canyon in Arizona. They used the water from Cataract Creek to raise crops throughout the summer months. After their final harvest, they climbed out of the canyon and moved to its rim. There, they gathered piñon and juniper fruits and hunted pumas, deer, and mountain sheep. The Havasupai lived in pole-framed lodges or in natural or dug-out stone shelters.

Yavapai

The Yavapai, whose name comes from a word that means "people of the sun" or "crooked-mouth people," were enemies of the Walapai. The two nations often engaged in battle. In the southernmost parts of their territory, some Yavapai were able to grow small crops of maize and tobacco, but they were mainly hunter-gatherers. Carrying few possessions, they often traveled between 20 and 40 miles (32-64 km) on foot each day in search of food. At their campsites, they built wickiups for shelter. The Yavapai were skillful basket makers. Some also made pottery.

Walapai

The Walapai farmed when possible, but they had access only to small plots of land with little water. They built temporary wickiups and domed lodges. They made baskets of many shapes and sizes, in which they gathered and dried foods. They even made baskets that could hold water, as shown right, by sealing them with **pitch**. Pitch was made from pine sap. The Walapai were also known as "pine tree people."

The Navajo

The Navajo (Navaho) call themselves Dineh (Diné), which means "the people." The first Navajo peoples in the Southwest probably arrived during the 1400s. They migrated, along with the Apache people, from the far north—probably present-day Canada. They settled near the Pueblo peoples in what is now northwestern New Mexico and northeastern Arizona. The Navajo built seasonal hogans and lived close to their family members. They survived as nomadic hunter-gatherers, who sometimes raided neighboring pueblos to take food, clothing, and goods.

Learning from neighbors

As the Navajo became familiar with Pueblo culture, they began to adopt a new way of life. They began farming where they could. From the Pueblo peoples, they learned how to weave cloth and to make pottery and baskets. The Navajo copied the looms on which the Pueblo peoples wove cloth and blankets and soon developed their own style of weaving.

Other visitors

After Spanish settlers arrived, the Navajo began to acquire sheep and goats from the Europeans. They soon began to raise flocks of sheep for milk, wool, and meat. Wool became especially important to the Navajo, as they became skilled weavers famous for their blankets and rugs. They supported themselves by trading these goods with other nations.

The Navajo used fibers colored with natural dyes to weave beautiful patterns and designs into cloth, blankets, and rugs. They developed a style of weaving that is now recognized all over the world.

The Apache

The Apache, like the Navajo, lived a nomadic lifestyle of hunting and gathering. Their ancestors traveled with the Navajo from the north to New Mexico and Arizona, around the year 1400. In their own language, the Apache have many names, such as Tineh, N'De, Haisndayin, and Deman, but all these names mean "the people." The Apache of the Southwest are divided into four smaller groups: the Jicarilla Apache, the Chiricahua Apache, the Mescalero Apache, and the Western Apache. Each of these groups was made up of several **bands**, or family groups. Apache peoples identified themselves by their bands.

Hunting and raiding

When they first arrived in the Southwest, the Apache relied on hunting animals such as deer and gathering plant foods such as cactus fruit. They did not store extra food when it was available, as many of their neighbors in farming villages did. When the Apache's food sources ran low, they often raided a nearby village and took food as well as goods such as clothing.

The "Apache fiddle" was an instrument made from a painted yucca stalk. It was played with a bow made of wood and sinew.

(left) Apache moccasins had high tops and often curled over at the toe.

The Apache, like most other Southwest nations, acquired horses from the Spanish and from Plains nations to the north, such as the Comanche. Hunters soon came to appreciate the speed with which they could travel on horseback.

Neighboring nations

Many nations from neighboring regions made regular visits to the Southwest. Nations from the Great Plains and present-day Mexico, California, and Texas all traveled to this region. The Ute, Southern Paiute, Comanche, Yeomem (Yaqui), and Baja California Yumans had many reasons to travel to the Southwest. They visited friends and allies and gathered resources. The most important reason, however, was for trade.

Trading allowed sedentary nations to obtain items such as wood, meat, hides, and shells from distant locations. Nomadic peoples could trade these items with farmers for seeds, crops, baskets, and woven cloth. Nations also exchanged knowledge of farming methods and skills such as weaving, pottery making, and basket making. They shared news about distant family members and other nations and compared hunting routes.

Nomadic peoples traveled great distances to trade with other groups.

Keeping in touch

Many nations outside the region felt strong bonds with the nations in the Southwest. For example, the Southern Paiute felt deeply tied to the Hopi, and the Baja Yuman speakers had kinship ties with their Yuman-speaking cousins. If these nations were troubled by war or hunger, they could often call on their distant relations for food or other assistance.

Hunting territories

Although many nations shared ties, relations among Southwest nations and their neighbors were sometimes tense. Some Southwest nations sent hunting parties into the territories of the Plains nations to bring back bison. The hunters had to travel in large groups in order to protect themselves from the nations whose homelands they were invading.

These Comanche scouts are sharing news gathered in the Southwest.

A changing world

Europeans first arrived in the Southwest in the 1500s, when Spanish explorers and Christian **missionaries** entered the region and tried to settle there. Some nations were barely visited by the Spanish, whereas others were invaded by them. Almost all nations were affected in some way, however. The Spanish carried diseases that were new to the Native peoples, whose bodies could not fight the illnesses. The diseases spread quickly, and many Native people died as a result.

Most Southwest nations openly rebelled against Spanish control at some point in time. In 1680, many Pueblo groups joined together and revolted. They fought a bloody battle and succeeded in driving the settlers away from Pueblo territories for several years. The most famous resisters, however, were the Apache. They fought tirelessly and gained a notorious reputation among the Spanish, Mexicans, and, later, the Americans, who wanted to remove them from their territories.

One of the first Spanish explorers in the Southwest was Francisco Vasquez de Coronado, whose party is shown above. When he arrived at one of the pueblos on the Rio Grande, he demanded food and supplies for his troops. Soon supplies began to run low, and the Pueblo people protested. Many were executed for resisting the Spanish.

Persecution

The nations of the Southwest lived on land that fell under Spanish, Mexican, and American rule between the 1500s and 1800s. During that time, the newcomers demanded land, loyalty, labor, and goods from the Native peoples whose homelands they had invaded. They also persecuted Native people who refused to give up their spiritual beliefs. Children were taken from their families and sent to boarding schools, where they were not allowed to learn about their cultures. Entire groups of Native people were forced to live on **reservations**, or small parcels of land, that were far from their homelands.

Europeans introduced animals such as horses, sheep, and cattle, crops such as wheat, and a number of fruits and vegetables to the Southwest nations. These new animals and plants helped many people survive. The Navajo, for example, began to build an economy based on raising sheep.

The nations today

The Native nations of the Southwest were able to keep much of their land and culture, in spite of efforts by Europeans and Americans to change their lifestyles and spiritual beliefs. Many of the nations continue to thrive in the Southwest. Their descendants often speak the traditional languages and create beautiful arts and crafts in traditional ways. Most reservations now have cultural centers where visitors can learn about past and present Native cultures and purchase the work of Native artists. If you would like to learn more about the Southwest, Native history, or Native peoples today, there are several great websites to visit. Try:

- www.cinprograms.org/index.html
- www.swirc.org
- www.newmexico.org/culture/indian culture.html

(below) Southwest artist Ben Billy creates beautiful pottery.

Glossary

Note: Boldfaced terms that are defined in the text may not appear in the glossary.

descendant A person related to ancient peoples through bloodlines

flood farmer A farmer who relies on floods of water, such as heavy rainfall, to water crops

hunter-gatherer A name given to a person who lives a nomadic lifestyle of hunting and gathering

irrigation A method of directing water through ditches and canals from a water source, such as a river, to a crop field

language family A group of languages that have similar features or origins

mesa A raised table of land

missionary A person who travels from place to place to convert people to a different faith

nation A group of Native people with a common language, culture, and history

nomadic Describing a lifestyle in which people move from one location to the next, never staying in a permanent settlement

pigment A natural coloring agent

pithouse A dwelling of the ancient Southwest cultures that was dug out of the ground and covered by mats

plateau A flat table of land

pueblo A large apartment-style structure made of stone or adobe bricks

ramada A pole and brush shelter used for shade in warm weather

reservation A parcel of land, chosen by the government, where a Native nation lives

sedentary Describing a lifestyle that involves living in a permanent settlement year-round

seminomadic Describing a lifestyle that involves staying in a settlement for only part of the year

tributary A stream or small river that feeds into a larger river

Index